P9-DNG-073

BAS RELIEF
& APPLIQUE

LESLEY HERBERT
CONSULTANT · LINDSAY JOHN BRADSHAW

MEREHURST

I dedicate this book to the bakery staff and students (past and present) at Barking College,
England for all their help, friendship and laughter.
Special thanks to Lillian Dowding and Peter Whiteley for their confidence and encouragement.

≈

Published in 1991 by Merehurst Limited, Ferry House,
51-57 Lacy Road, Putney, London SW15 1PR.

Copyright © Merehurst Limited 1991

ISBN 1 85391 221 2

All rights reserved. No part of this publication may be reproduced,
stored in a retrieval system, or transmitted in any form or by any
means, electronic, mechanical, photocopying, recording or otherwise
without the prior written permission of the copyright owner.
A catalogue record of this book is available from the British Library.

Edited by Jenni Fleetwood
Designed by Peter Bridgewater
Photography by David Gill
Colour Separation by Fotographics Ltd,
UK - Hong Kong
Printed by Proost International Book Production,
Turnhout, Belgium

The author and publishers would like to thank the following students
for producing the cakes in this book: Audrey Bailey (p19, 65); Sue
Ballard (p11); Christine Berry (p43, 65); Jo Flight (p35, 65); Audrey
Harris (p27, 51, 65); Jean Hodgkinson (p59, 65); Carol Mintz (p33,
63); Maureen Newman (p23); Sheila Nicholls (p47); Sandra Nutley
(p53); Deirdre Perkins (p39); Pat Saunders (p29).

Thanks are also due to the following suppliers:
Orchard Products, 49 Langdale Road, Hove, East Sussex, BN3 4HR;
Simon Elvin Ltd, Wooburn Industrial Park, Wooburn Green, Bucks
HP10 0PE; Cel Cakes, Springfield House, Gate Helmsley, York YO4
1NF; Twins Wedding Shop, Victoria Road, Romford, Essex RM1 2LT.

NOTES ON USING THE RECIPES
For all recipes, quantities are given in metric, Imperial and cup
measurements. Follow one set of measures only as they are not
interchangeable. Standard 5ml teaspoons (tsp) and 15ml tablespoons (tbsp) are used. Australian readers, whose tablespoons
measure 20ml, should adjust quantities accordingly. All spoon
measures are assumed to be level unless otherwise stated.
Ovens should be pre-heated to specified temperature.
Eggs are a standard size 3 unless otherwise stated.
Quantities of icing used on cakes are approximate.

CONTENTS

INTRODUCTION

*B*as Relief and Appliqué are exciting techniques which have now been used in cake decorating for decades. In sugarcraft terms, the techniques are very similar: in both cases the figure is built up by cutting out shapes and applying them to the cake or plaque.

Appliqué is a very effective method of decorating. Shapes of flowers or figures are cut out of finely rolled modelling paste and secured to the cake. The shapes can be enhanced by piping small stitches or by using brush embroidery around the edges. The technique owes its origins to needlework. Appliqué is a French term which has been defined as a decoration or trimming of one material sewn or otherwise fixed onto another.

In sugarcraft, bas relief involves padding a figure with paste to achieve a three-dimensional effect as opposed to the flat appliqué style. This term has also been borrowed (somewhat loosely) from another craft, namely sculpture, where it is used to indicate a design that is raised from the background. In bas relief (low relief/basso-relievo) the figure projects only slightly and no part is entirely detached. In demi relief (half relief/mezzo-relievo) the figure is more prominent.

The aim of this book is to demonstrate how almost any theme or figure can be made using cut-out shapes which can be applied to the sides or top of any shape of cake. In order to explore as many avenues as possible, the book was compiled with the help of a talented group of advanced students at Barking College of Technology, England. Although all of a similar high standard, the cakes thus represent a wide range of styles and incorporate diverse techniques.

Working with the author, a lecturer at the college, the students addressed a variety of problems associated with this sugarcraft skill. The solutions they arrived at are revealed in the chapter on cake designs. Recipes which contain new techniques or highlight special skills are illustrated with step-by-step photographs, which should be looked at in conjunction with methods.

As even a cursory glance at this book reveals, bas relief and appliqué are techniques that lend themselves to an infinite variety of cake designs, from the reproducing of a picture of a well-loved pet to the creation of a delicate strawberry fairy.

ROYAL ICING

❖

The easiest way to make perfect royal icing is by using the *weight* ratio 1:6 for egg white and sugar. It is for this reason that a solid measure is given for the egg white in the recipe that follows.

125g (4 oz/¾ cup) egg white
750g (1½ lb/4½ cups) icing (confectioners')
sugar, sifted

Put egg white in a grease-free bowl. Add three quarters of the icing (confectioners') sugar and beat with an electric mixer for 2 minutes on slow speed. Adjust consistency with remaining sugar and beat for 3 minutes more on slow speed until icing peaks. Cover bowl with a damp cloth to prevent icing drying and forming a crust. Makes about 750g/1½ lb.

NOTE Powdered albumen may be used. Reconstitute it in the proportion of 90g (3 oz/⅓ cup) to 600ml (1 pint/2½ cups) water.

FLOWER PASTE

❖

500g (1 lb/3 cups) icing (confectioners') sugar
1 sheet leaf gelatine
2 tsp white vegetable fat (shortening)
2 tsp liquid glucose
1 tsp gum tragacanth
4 tsp CMC (high viscosity carboxymethyl
cellulose)
1-1¼ medium egg whites

Put icing (confectioners') sugar in a heatproof bowl, covering surface closely with greaseproof paper (parchment) to prevent formation of a crust. Warm in a 150°C (300°F/Gas 2) oven. Meanwhile soak gelatine in a large bowl of water for 5 minutes until pliable. Remove gelatine from water and place in a small heatproof bowl with fat and glucose. Stand bowl over a saucepan of hot (not boiling) water and stir until dissolved. Mix warmed icing sugar, gum tragacanth and CMC in warm dry bowl and add 1 egg white, with gelatine mixture. Begin mixing on slow speed. Increase mixer speed and beat until paste is white and pliable, adding more egg white if necessary. Store in a clean polythene bag in an airtight container for 24 hours before use or freeze until required. Makes about 500g (1 lb).

SUGARPASTE

❖

Commercial sugarpaste is a highly satisfactory product and was used for all the cakes in this book. To make your own sugarpaste, follow the recipe on page 24.

Experienced sugarcraft artists will already have much of the equipment required for bas relief and appliqué. Some of the more useful items, illustrated opposite are (clockwise from left): knives*, scalpel, palette knife*, straight edge*, side scraper*, smoother*, airbrush, letter moulds, greaseproof paper (parchment)*, wax paper*, non-stick rolling pin and boards*, parsley/herb cutter, tracing wheel, wooden dowel, veining tool, bone/ball tool, scissors*, flower cutters, straight and round Garrett frill cutters, crimpers, foam, piping tubes (tips), clay gun, brushes*, pins*, cocktail sticks (toothpicks), scalloped edge cutters and dusting powder (petal dust/blossom tint).

NOTE *Items marked with an asterisk (*) are not included in equipment lists in recipes. You will also need thin card for templates.*

MODELLING PASTE

❖

Most of the bas relief and appliqué in this book has been created from this versatile paste. It can be coloured in various ways, rolled very thinly, moulded by hand or shaped in a clay gun. For perfect results, it is worth taking the time to master a few basic techniques. The photographs on this page clearly show how a clay gun may be used to maximum effect, and the use of dusting powder (petal dust/blossom tint) on dry paste figures. Opposite, instructions are given for making frills and pleats, and moulding hands and arms. See also Expert Advice, page 26.

60g (2 oz) Flower Paste (page 6)
60g (2 oz) Sugarpaste (page 24)

In a clean dry bowl, knead the two pastes together until pliable. Place in a polythene bag and store in an airtight container. Makes 125g (4 oz).

EXPERT ADVICE

≈

COLOURING To colour modelling paste, knead in paste colours or dusting powder (petal dust/blossom tint). Concentrated liquid colours may be used but may make the paste sticky. Dusting powder may be used on dry figures to highlight areas as described right.
STORAGE Refrigerate in small polythene bags inside airtight containers. Wrap coloured paste separately. Coloured paste becomes sticky during storage due to the glycerol (glycerine) in the colour. If necessary, knead in extra icing (confectioners') sugar.
USAGE Knead a small piece of paste, the size of a walnut, until smooth and pliable. Roll out paste on a lightly greased board; do not use cornflour (cornstarch) or icing (confectioners') sugar as these may cause the paste to dry out too quickly. Keep unused paste covered with polythene to prevent it drying.

CLAY GUN *This useful modelling tool comes with a selection of tops to create various shapes. To use, soften some modelling paste with vegetable fat, place in gun and push down to extrude paste. Twisting paste can introduce a variety of effects.*

USING DUSTING POWDER *These fine powders come in a range of colours and can be mixed together or with cornflour (cornstarch) to provide background colour, create special effects, or shade leaves or blossoms. Mask areas to be kept free of colour. Between colours, clean brush on dry absorbent kitchen paper.*

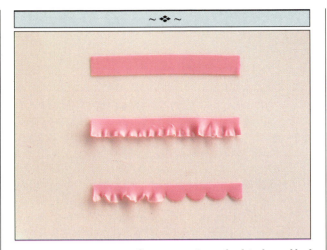

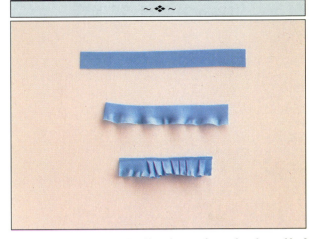

MAKING A FRILL *Cut a strip of thinly-rolled modelling paste. Frill by rolling a smooth wooden cocktail stick (toothpick) along one edge. If splits occur, it may be because paste was too thick or cocktail stick had become sticky. An alternative finish may be achieved with a straight Garrett frill cutter.*

MAKING PLEATS *Frill edge of a thinly-rolled strip of modelling paste as described left. Then, holding paste in your left hand, gently mould it into pleats, using finger and thumb of your right hand. Place pleated paste on a board and trim top edge straight with a knife.*

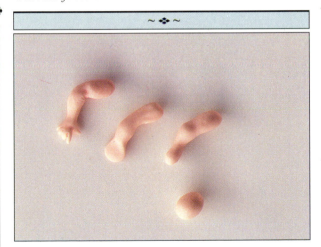

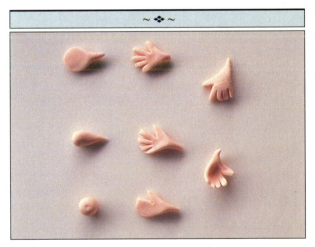

MOULDING AN ARM *Using a suitably-sized ball of flesh-coloured modelling paste, roll into a sausage shape with your index finger. Shape wrist and elbow by applying slightly more pressure to these areas, then model a little hand. For fine moulding, follow instructions right.*

MOULDING A HAND *Roll a small ball of flesh-coloured modelling paste into a tear-drop shape and flatten end. Cut a V-shape from one side to create a thumb, then make three more cuts and separate fingers, gently pinching tips together. Smooth paste between your finger and thumb, place tiny hand on soft sponge and cup palm with a ball tool.*

BIRTHDAY CAKE
WITH APPLIQUE TRAIN

*T*his attractive design can be adapted to use on any number or letter shaped cake.

---

number three shape cake
apricot glaze
1kg (2 lb) marzipan (almond paste)
clear alcohol (gin or vodka)
1.75kg (3½ lb) Sugarpaste, see page 24
selection of food colourings
small amount of Royal Icing, see page 6
185g (6 oz) Modelling Paste, see page 8
EQUIPMENT
35 x 40cm (14 x 16 in) cake board
no. 3 and 42 piping tubes (tips)
scalpel
embossing tool or textured button
flower cutter

● Brush cake with apricot glaze. Marzipan top and sides in separate pieces. Dampen marzipan with alcohol. Colour half sugarpaste pale blue; roll out and cover cake. Gently tuck sugarpaste into sides and smooth. Cover board with white sugarpaste. When dry, attach cake to board.

● Trace train templates below and cut out of thin card. Colour half the royal icing black. Using a no. 3 piping tube (tip), pipe a line around the base of cake. Pipe bulbs of icing on the piped line about 1cm (½ in) apart to represent the track.

● Brightly colour small pieces of modelling paste, leaving some white. Working with one colour at a time, roll out modelling paste on a lightly greased board. Using templates and scalpel, cut out basic engine shape and sufficient carriages to go all round the cake. Neaten wheel arches with end of a piping tube (tip). Dampen back of paste shapes with water and secure to side of cake.

● Cut out funnel and carriage motifs from thinly rolled modelling paste, varying motifs if liked. Make wheels by cutting paste circles with the end of a piping tube (tip). Texture each wheel with an embossing tool or textured button. Dampen funnel, carriage motifs and wheels and fix to cake.

● Make smoke clouds by cutting large flowers from white modelling paste. Stretch shapes by gently rolling them with a non-stick rolling pin. Attach shapes to top of cake. Finally, finish top of cake by piping an S- and C-scroll border using a no. 1 tube (tip) and white royal icing.

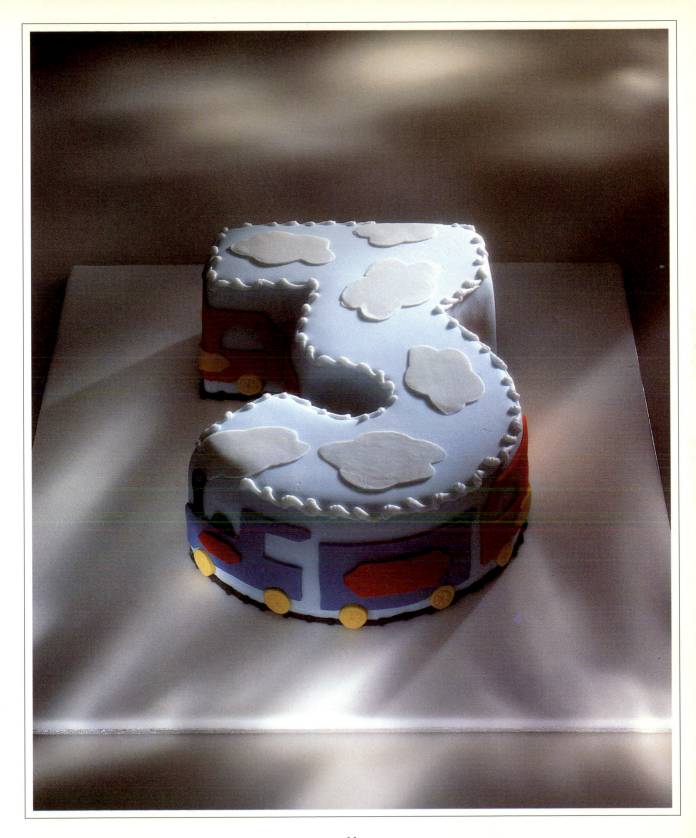

BASKET CAKE WITH BRUSH-EMBROIDERED APPLIQUE FLOWERS

*T*he technique used for the appliqué flowers can be adapted for a variety of different blooms, such as roses, sweet peas or peonies. Try cutting the flowers from white paste and using different colours for the brush embroidery. The method below is amplified in step-by-step instructions on pages 14-15.

20 x 15cm (8 x 6 in) oval cake
apricot glaze
1 kg (2 lb) marzipan (almond paste)
clear alcohol (gin or vodka)
1.25kg (2½ lb) Sugarpaste, see page 24
small amount of Royal Icing, see page 6
selection of food colourings
Flower Paste, see page 6
clear piping gel
egg white
confectioners' glaze
8 pink and yellow sugar carnations
E Q U I P M E N T
28 x 23cm (11 x 9 in) cake board
scriber
no. 0, 3 and 1 piping tubes (tips)
scalpel
ivy leaf cutter
clay gun

○ Brush cake with apricot glaze. Cover with marzipan (almond paste) and brush with clear alcohol. Coat cake and board with sugarpaste, smooth and leave for 3 days to dry.

○ Scribe and pipe the stems for the flowers on the side of the cake, following step 1 on page 14. Using a no. 3 piping tube (tip) and dark green royal icing, pipe a border on the cake base.

○ Trace one flower from template below and cut out of thin card. Colour small pieces of flower paste pink and yellow. Working with one colour at a time, roll out paste. Using template and scalpel, cut out flowers for side of cake, see step 2, page 15. Colour flower paste green and cut out and attach ivy leaves following step 3, page 15.

○ Mix royal icing with clear piping gel, see Expert Advice, page 14 and embroider all ivy leaves and flowers, following steps 4 and 5. When duplicate flowers are dry, attach them to cake as described in step 6.

○ Trace 'Best Wishes' inscription and scribe it on top of cake. Using a no. 0 tube (tip) and green royal icing, pipe lettering. Trace basket template on page 14 and cut out of thin card. Colour some flower paste brown and mould a small cushion to pad out the basket shape. Dampen back with water and secure it to cake. Using template, accurately cut out silhouette of basket base. Dampen and attach to cake over paste cushion.

Continued on page 14

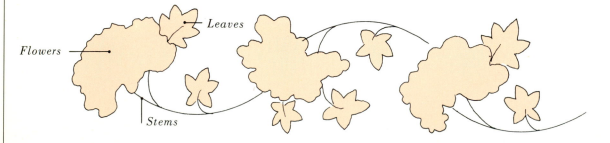

Flowers — Leaves — Stems

Continued from page 12

● Soften some brown flower paste with vegetable fat, (shortening) and extrude it through the clay gun, see page 8, twisting paste to form a rope. Paint egg white along top and bottom edge of basket and secure paste rope trim, then extrude another piece of paste, about 10cm (4 in) long for handle. Fix it in place, allow basket to dry, then varnish with confectioners' glaze. Arrange sugar carnations and reserved ivy leaves in basket, attaching them with royal icing.

Best Wishes

EXPERT ADVICE

≈

To slow down speed at which royal icing sets, mix it with clear piping gel in the proportion 250ml (8 fl oz/1 cup) icing to 1 tsp gel.

~ 1 ~

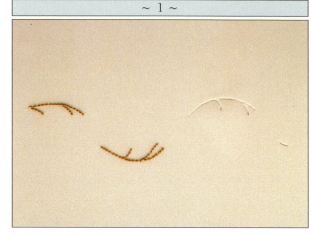

Measure height and circumference of cake and make a greaseproof paper (parchment) template for side. Trace stem design only from sketch on page 12 onto paper template, repeating design and adjusting length if necessary. Scribe design on cake. Using no. 0 piping tube (tip) and dark green royal icing, pipe small shells for stems.

~ 4 ~

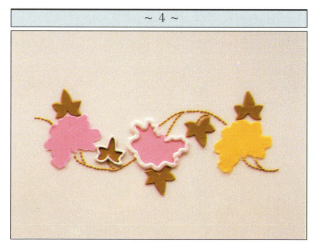

Mix royal icing with piping jelly, see left. Brush embroider flowers and leaves on side of cake; also reserved flowers and leaves. Work on one flower or leaf at a time, as icing will not brush smoothly once it begins to dry. Begin by piping outline of flower or leaf, using a no. 1 piping tube (tip); apply firm pressure for larger flowers.

~ 2 ~

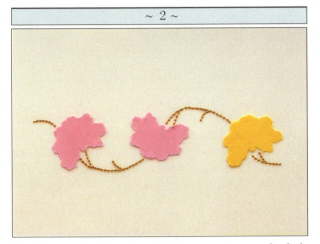

Roll out suitably tinted flower paste on a lightly greased board. Using template and scalpel, cut out flowers for side of cake. Dampen backs lightly with water and attach to stems on side of cake. Cut out duplicate set of flowers; leave on a flat board to dry.

~ 3 ~

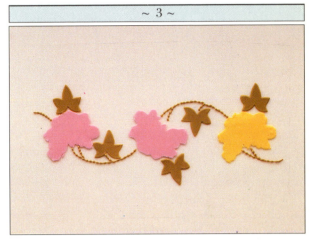

Using green food colouring with a small amount of black, colour some flower paste a dark mossy green. Roll out paste as thinly as possible on a lightly greased board. Cut out leaves for side of cake, using ivy leaf cutter. Attach to stems while still pliable. Cut out nine extra leaves for top of cake; reserve on a board.

~ 5 ~

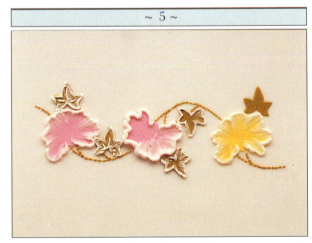

Using a damp paintbrush, brush icing onto petals or centre of leaf, leaving icing thicker around the edge and brushing it thinly enough to allow the colour of the flower or leaf to be seen through the icing. Keep brush clean and damp; if too wet it will be difficult to brush icing without dissolving it. Always brush from edge to centre.

~ 6 ~

When all brush-embroidered flowers and leaves have dried, attach duplicate set of flowers to cake. Pipe a small bulb of well-beaten icing onto the back of each flower. Marry it to its partner, fixing it to the cake at a slight angle to create a three dimensional effect. Reserve remaining brush embroidered leaves for top of cake.

FLOWER PLAQUES

Appliqué plaques are highly effective as a form of decoration. Easier to work on than cakes, they have the added advantage that they can be angled on the cake for clear visibility - and removed before the cake is cut as a tangible reminder of the occasion.

The flowers displayed on the plaques are all variations on appliqué, whereas leaves are painted directly onto the coating surface. Melt a small amount of vegetable fat (shortening) in a small bowl. Create a palette by placing small mounds of green, brown, yellow and skin-tone dusting powder (petal dust/blossom tint) on a dinner plate set over a bowl of warm water. Mix dusting powder with a drop of hot fat. When required depth of colour has been reached, paint leaves on plaque, mixing colours if liked to create natural-looking foliage. The advantage of this method is that delicate colours can be created. Liquid colours are often very bright and may run if the surface is absorbent.

ANEMONES Trace design on page 67, scribe it on plaque and paint leaves. Cut out card templates of each flower silhouette. Begin with flower that appears to be furthest away. Roll out pink Modelling Paste, see page 8, as thinly as possible on a lightly greased board. Using template and scalpel, cut out flower shape. Mark petals with wide end of veining tool, working from outer edge of each petal towards centre. Dampen plaque lightly and position flower silhouette. Make card templates for petals that are raised from the background, see illustration opposite. Cut out petals, texture them by marking several lines with narrow end of veining tool; attach to flower. Make all flowers in the same way. For each centre, flatten a small ball of black paste and texture with veining tool. Pipe small dots of yellow icing round each flower centre to represent stamens. Pipe or paint card and inscription.

DAFFODILS Scribe design on page 67 on plaque and paint leaves. Cut out card templates of flower sections. Roll out yellow Modelling Paste and cut out the three back petals, using template and scalpel. Mark lines on petals with veining tool. Dampen plaque lightly and attach back petals. Repeat for two side petals. Cut out trumpet in two pieces, frilling edge of oval shape with a cocktail stick (toothpick). Build up flower shape by placing the petals directly on top of each other. Using same technique as for leaves, make up yellow and orange dusting powder colour and paint daffodils - the added fat will give them a realistic waxy appearance.

PANSIES These are made in much the same way as the anemones, but instead of building up shape by adding extra petals, detail is provided by brush embroidery. Scribe design on page 67 on plaque; paint leaves. Pipe curve, using a no. 1 tube (tip) and white royal icing. Cut card templates of pansies from blue Modelling Paste, see page 8; attach to plaque. Using a no. 2 piping tube and white royal icing, outline edge of petal which appears furthest away. Make up dilute solutions of food colouring in several toning shades. Dip brush in food colouring, then brush icing over petal as described on pages 14-15. Continue to outline one petal at a time until both flowers are complete. Paint a little black colour on the bottom petal of each flower. Pipe centres, using white royal icing.

ROSES Each rose is made up of three layers of petals. After scribing design on page 67 and making card templates for petals, paint leaves on plaque. Cut back petals from pink Modelling Paste, page 8. Attach to lightly dampened plaque. Cut out two more layers of petals; leave on a board to dry. Using white royal icing, brush embroider around the edge of all petals, including those on plaque. pages 14-15. When icing is completely dry, assemble roses, securing each layer of petals with royal icing. Pipe a small bulb of yellow icing in the centre of each and surround with tiny dots for stamens. Complete the picture with small white paste flowers cut out using a primrose cutter; pipe or paint card and inscription.

CHRISTMAS CAKE
WITH BAS RELIEF CANDLES

*T*his beautiful cake illustrates just how effective bas relief can be. Step-by-step instructions for the candles are on pages 20-21.

18cm (7 in) round cake
apricot glaze
1kg (2 lb) marzipan (almond paste)
1kg (2 lb) Royal Icing, see page 6
selection of food colourings
60g (2 oz) Modelling Paste, see page 8
selection of dusting powders
(petal dust/blossom tints)
vegetable fat (shortening)
Flower Paste, see page 6
E Q U I P M E N T
comb scraper
25cm (10 in) round gold cake board
no. 44, 42, 2 and 1 piping tubes (tips)
scalpel
veining tool
holly, blossom and leaf cutters
ball tool

● Brush cake with apricot glaze and cover with marzipan (almond paste). Coat with cream-coloured royal icing, smoothing the surface with a straight edge and side scraper. Use the comb scraper (see diagram right for pattern) to mark the final coat on the side. Attach cake to board. Run out inscription on page 20 on wax paper; see page 38 for technique. Allow to dry completely, then paint with gold colour.

● Divide top edge of cake into 8 equal sections. Using a no. 44 tube (tip) and full peak royal icing, pipe scrolls on top and bottom edges. Overpipe scrolls using no. 42 and 2 tubes.

● Make bas relief candles, following instructions on pages 20-21. Attach candles to cake with royal icing. Using white flower paste and large blossom cutter, cut out Christmas roses. Colour some

modelling paste green and cut out six holly leaves. Smooth edges with a ball tool. If liked, edges may be lightly brushed with dusting powder to give a realistic effect. Twist holly slightly to create shape. Attach holly leaves and Christmas roses to cake with royal icing, see step 6, page 21. Using no. 1 piping tube (tip) and red royal icing, pipe small dots to represent berries.

● Roll out remaining green modelling paste and cut out 16 more holly leaves. Secure leaves, in pairs, at equal intervals around side of cake. Pipe two red berries between each pair of leaves. Remove run-out letters from wax paper and secure to cake with dots of royal icing.

Comb Scraper

Making the bas relief candles illustrated on previous page

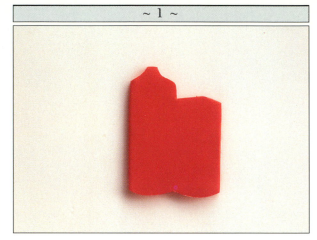

~ 1 ~

Trace template (left) and cut the silhouette of the candles out of thin card. The template is 2.5mm (1/8 in) smaller than the completed design. Colour a small piece of modelling paste red and roll it out on a lightly greased board. Using template and scalpel, cut out silhouette of candles. Dampen back and position on cake.

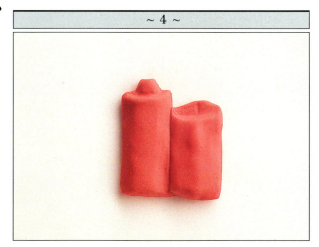

~ 4 ~

Cut out a second silhouette, slightly larger than the first. Dampen the back of the paste and place over the built-up candles. Smooth the edges to cover the base, then use the wide end of the veining tool to smooth and shape the tops.

~ 2 ~

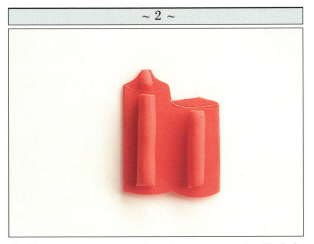

Roll out two ropes of red paste, each slightly shorter than the candles on the silhouette. Model a tear drop shape for each candle top. Dampen the silhouette on the cake slightly and attach the ropes of paste. These will form the padding for the bas relief.

~ 3 ~

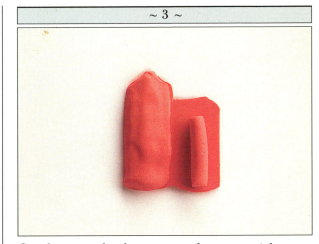

Gently smooth the ropes of paste with your fingertips. Smooth down the edges, leaving the centres thicker than the sides.

~ 5 ~

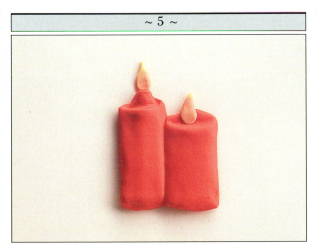

Use the leaf cutter to cut out the flames. Dust them with yellow dusting powder at the top and orange at the bottom. Allow to dry, then attach to candles with a spot of royal icing. Brush candles with a thin coat of melted vegetable fat (shortening) to create a wax effect.

~ 6 ~

Using a no. 1 tube (tip) and softened royal icing, pipe three lines on each candle for the small candles. Top each with a small shell to represent the flame. When dry, paint small candles gold. Make holly leaves and Christmas roses, see page 18. Attach to cake, dust flower centres with green dusting powder and pipe on yellow icing dots for stamens.

HEXAGONAL CAKE
WITH BAS RELIEF DOG

*T*he technique used here can easily be adapted for different animals. Step-by-step instructions for making the bas relief dog are given on pages 24-25.

23cm (9 in) hexagonal cake (measured point to point)
apricot glaze
1.5kg (3 lb) marzipan (almond paste)
clear alcohol (gin or vodka)
1.5kg (3 lb) Sugarpaste, see page 24
selection of food colourings
Royal Icing, see page 6
Flower Paste, see page 6
egg white
E Q U I P M E N T
28cm (11 in) hexagonal cake board
(measured point to point)
scriber
no.1 and 0 piping tubes (tips)
small and medium blossom cutters
block of foam
ball tool
parsley cutter
scalpel
veining tool

● Brush cake with apricot glaze and cover with marzipan (almond paste). Brush with alcohol. Colour three quarters of the sugarpaste pink, roll out and coat cake. Place on board and leave to dry for three days.

● Make a greaseproof paper (parchment) template for one side of the cake. Cut it to a scallop design and scribe it on the side of the cake. Repeat the pattern on the remaining five sides. Using white royal icing and no. 1 tube (tip) pipe a small shell border around the base of the cake.

● Roll out some white flower paste as thinly as possible on a lightly greased board. Using the cutters, cut out about 60 small and 30 larger blossoms and place them on the foam block. Cup centres with ball tool and leave to dry.

● To make bows, cut twelve 7.5cm (3 in) strips of thin white flower paste, using the parsley cutter. Brush egg white on the centre of one strip and fold the ends over to form the loops. Take a second strip of paste, fold it in half, and cut tails into V-shapes. Assemble bows with egg white and leave to dry. Attach blossoms to side of cake with royal icing, following the scribed line and varying the size of the blossoms to create a garland effect. Fix a bow at top of each scallop, as shown opposite.

● Make bas relief dog directly on the surface of the cake, using template below and following instructions on pages 24-25. Finally pipe the grass and embroidery on top of the cake, using softened white royal icing and no.0 tube (tip).

BAS RELIEF ANIMALS

❖

The bas relief dog would delight any animal lover, but if the recipient of your cake has a different type of pet, the design can easily be adapted. A horse or greyhound might be appropriate for the sport enthusiast, while an ardent conservationist might appreciate a whale. Simply photocopy a picture or photograph of the animal, enlarging it if necessary to a suitable size. The figure is built up directly on the cake, with prominent areas padded to create a three dimensional effect.

The dog template on page 22 shows all the areas to be padded, but it is not difficult to identify the key areas on a photograph or picture. The parts of the animal that appear closest to you will require building up.

Study the photograph or picture to determine how the fur texture should be marked. Do not be tempted to cut out all the pieces at once as the paste may dry too quickly to texture the fur.

EXPERT ADVICE

≈

Although excellent sugarpaste is available commercially, it can be made at home: Mix 60g (2 oz/¼ cup) sugar with 45g (1½ oz/3 tbsp) liquid glucose, 15g (¼ oz/1 tbsp) white vegetable fat (shortening) and 1 tbsp water in a small saucepan. Bring to the boil, then stir in 7g (¼ oz/1 envelope) powdered gelatine. When dissolved, remove pan from heat and stir in 45g (1½ oz/¼ cup) Royal Icing, see page 6. Tip mixture into a bowl and sift in 375g (12 oz/2¼ cups) icing (confectioners') sugar. Mix with a palette knife, then knead to a firm paste. Wrap sugarpaste in a polythene bag and store in an airtight container. Makes 500g (1 lb).

~ 1 ~

Trace silhouette of dog on page 22 and cut a template from thin card. Mix remaining sugarpaste with an equal amount of flower paste to make modelling paste. Roll out some of the paste on a lightly greased board. Using template and scalpel, cut out the dog silhouette. Dampen back of paste with water and secure it to the cake.

~ 4 ~

While paste is still supple, mark fur texture with a veining tool. Texturing will stretch the paste slightly to cover the base padding completely.

~ 2 ~

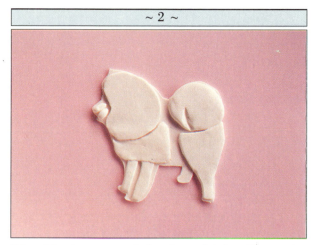

Identify the parts of the dog which will require building up. These are marked on the illustration on page 22. Cut the pieces for the padding out of paste and secure them to the silhouette with egg white.

~ 3 ~

Cut out a second silhouette from the paste, paint the back with egg white and place it over the padded dog, smoothing it over with your fingertips. Mark the position for the ear and hollow the eye socket with the ball tool.

~ 5 ~

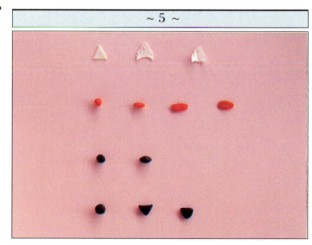

Make features. Cut a triangle of white paste for the ear, mark the fur texture and attach it to the dog with egg white. Shape the eye, nose and tongue from small balls of coloured paste, securing them to the dog with egg white.

~ 6 ~

If required, the dog may be lightly brushed with dusting powder or painted to highlight or create shadows.

ROCKING HORSE FIGURE

*T*his charming rocking horse illustrates how the bas relief method described on pages 24-25 can be used to create alternative figures.

Trace the rocking horse on page 70 and cut out a template from thin card. Roll out some white modelling paste on a lightly greased board. Using template and scalpel, cut out horse silhouette, ignoring mane, tail and rocker. Place silhouette on a flat surface (or dampen the back and put it straight onto the cake, if preferred).

Lightly dampen silhouette with water and pad entire body with paste, smoothing edges with your fingertips to create a half relief figure.

Cut out a second silhouette, about 2.5mm (⅛ in) larger than the first, from modelling paste. Place this over the padding, smoothing and stretching paste slightly so that it fits snugly. Cut off excess paste with a scalpel.

Make mane and tail by extruding pink and blue paste through a clay gun (see page 8) and attaching it to the lightly dampened horse's neck. If you do not have a clay gun, a similar effect may be achieved by pushing some softened paste through a fine wire sieve or strainer. When threads are the correct length, slide a knife under the paste to cut it off neatly.

Cut out three strips of red modelling paste for the bridle. Cut out ear from white paste and paint eye with black food colour. Cut rocker and saddle from suitably coloured paste, texture edges with a small heart shape cutter and secure in place. Using a small stars shape cutter and modelling paste in a contrasting colour, cut out about 25 stars. Fix them in position as shown opposite.

When horse is dry, mark a line across the bottom of each leg with a knife. Apply dusting powder in a pale blue lustre colour for the hooves, see page 8. Lightly dust the edges of the animal with the same colour to make the paste shine and bring life to the figure.

EXPERT ADVICE

≈

Making modelling paste can be quite a laborious business, largely because the flower paste that forms part of it is in itself time consuming to make. If preferred, Mexican paste may be substituted for flower paste: Sift 250g (8 oz/1½ cups) icing (confectioners') sugar and 3 tsp gum tragacanth onto a clean surface. Place 1 tsp liquid glucose and 2 tbsp cold water in the centre of the sugar. Mix with a palette knife, then knead to a paste. Store as for sugarpaste.

EASTER EGG CAKE
WITH BAS RELIEF BUNNY

*B*ake the cake in an egg-shaped mould. Before removing cake, slice it across top, so that when turned out, the bottom will be flat. Instructions for the bunny are on pages 30-31.

15 x 23cm (6 x 9 in) egg-shaped cake
apricot glaze
750g (1½ lb) marzipan (almond paste)
clear alcohol (gin or vodka)
750g (1½ lb) Sugarpaste, see page 24
selection of food colourings
125g (4 oz) Modelling Paste, see page 8
vegetable fat (shortening)
pink dusting powder (petal dust/blossom tint)
Royal Icing, see page 6
E Q U I P M E N T
25 x 33cm (10 x 13 in) oval cake board
scalpel
veining tool
clay gun fitted with trefoil tip
ball tool
no.1 and 42 piping tubes (tips)
small and medium plunger blossom cutters

● Brush cake with apricot glaze and cover with marzipan (almond paste). Brush with clear alcohol and coat with sugarpaste. Place on board. Trace door on page 30 and cut a template from thin card. Place template on freshly coated cake, cut through sugarpaste coating and remove door portion, exposing marzipan. Dry for three days.
● Colour some sugarpaste light brown. Roll out to same thickness as sugarpaste used for coating cake. Using template and scalpel, cut out door. Dampen back with water and place in gap on cake, siting it flush with sugarpaste coating. Add detail to door and make bas relief bunny directly on cake, following instructions on pages 30-31.
● Pipe flower stalks around base of cake and next to door, using no.1 tube (tip) and green royal

icing. Using small and medium blossom cutters, cut flowers for side and top of cake from blue modelling paste. Dampen backs of flowers with water and fix to cake as shown opposite. Complete flowers by piping a dot of icing in each centre. Mould the larger leaves and flowers to the right of the door from modelling paste; attach to cake. Pipe a small shell border around base of cake, using no.42 tube and green royal icing.
● Make sugar ribbon and bow from pink modelling paste. Cut thinly rolled paste into 1cm (½ in) wide strips. Attach one length over top of cake, offsetting it slightly to the left. Dampen lightly with water. Attach two shorter lengths for ribbon tails, cutting a V-shape in the end of each. Make two loops for the bow. Fix to cake, then cover centre of bow with another small strip of paste.

Making the door and Easter Bunny illustrated on previous page

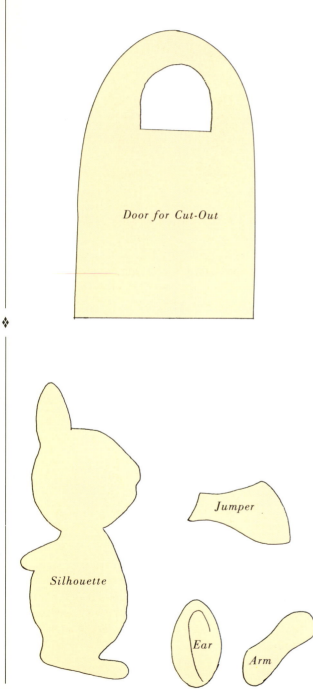

Door for Cut-Out

Silhouette

Jumper

Ear

Arm

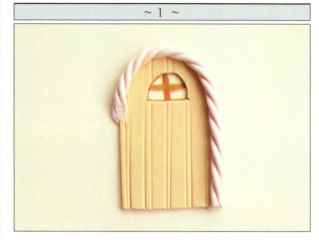

~ 1 ~

Using template and scalpel, cut out door from brown paste; position on cake. Texture lines in door using veining tool. Paint a cross to represent window. Soften some white or pink modelling paste with vegetable fat, place in clay gun, see page 8, and extrude a length of paste for door edge; twist, dampen back and secure to door.

~ 4 ~

Roll out some modelling paste. Using template and scalpel, cut out a second bunny silhouette, about 2.5mm ($\frac{1}{8}$ in) larger than the first. Dampen bunny on cake and place silhouette over padding, smoothing it into place and tucking the paste neatly into all the hollows. Mark small lines in direction of fur growth, using veining tool.

~ 2 ~

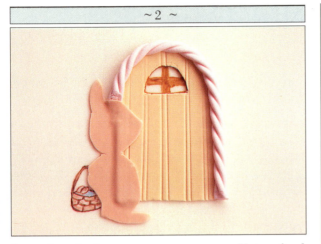

Smooth end of paste rope to neaten. Using food colouring and thin paintbrush, paint basket of eggs directly on cake coating. Trace Easter bunny silhouette, ear, arm and jumper left; cut out of thin card. Using template and scalpel, cut out bunny silhouette from thinly rolled modelling paste. Dampen back of paste; secure to cake.

~ 3 ~

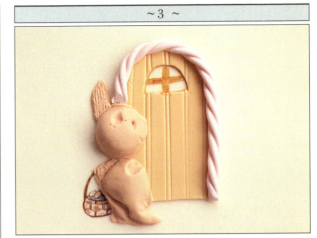

Pad body and head of bunny with modelling paste, using technique described on pages 24-25. Exaggerate eye, ear, arm and leg sockets, making hollows in paste with ball tool. Cut out back ear and arm from thinly rolled paste. Attach them to silhouette; texture fur (on back ear and arm only) with veining tool, see step 4, page 24.

~ 5 ~

Using template, scalpel and blue modelling paste, cut out jumper. Place on bunny and re-shape arm socket with ball tool. (Note that arm holes are avoided on bas relief figures where possible, to prevent raw edges showing.)

~ 6 ~

Model arm, front ear and tail. Dampen back of paste and attach pieces to bunny. Dust inside of ear with pink dusting powder. Texture tail with veining tool. Make eye and nose from tiny pieces of white paste, then paint eye detail with food colouring.

BAR MITZVAH CAKE

*A*Bar Mitzvah is always a cause for celebration. This cake recalls the solemnity of the occasion while adding a touch of humour that younger guests will appreciate.

20 x 33cm (8 x 13 in) book shape cake
apricot glaze
1.5kg (3 lb) marzipan (almond paste)
clear alcohol (gin or vodka)
2kg (4 lb) Sugarpaste, see page 24
selection of food colourings
500g (1 lb) Royal Icing, see page 6
125g (4 oz) Modelling Paste, see page 8
dusting powder (petal dust/blossom tint)
confectioners' varnish
clear piping gel
E Q U I P M E N T
33 x 43cm (13 x 7 in) cake board
crimper
no. 44 piping tube (tip)
scalpel
airbrush
ball tool

● Place cake on board. Brush with apricot glaze and cover with marzipan (almond paste). Brush with alcohol. Colour three quarters of the sugarpaste blue, roll it out and coat the cake. Smooth the surface. Texture the side of the cake with a sharp knife to represent the pages.
● Roll out remaining sugarpaste to a rectangle measuring 20 x 30cm (8 x 12 in). Dampen top of cake lightly with water. Position white paste on cake; crimp edges while paste is still pliable. Curl back two corners as shown right. Pipe a shell border around the base of the cake, using a no.44 piping tube (tip) and white royal icing.
● Using template on page 71, run out the Hebrew inscription Bar Mitzvah and the names on wax paper, using white royal icing, see Note, page 38.

When dry, paint silver. Position letters on cake top and attach with small dots of soft royal icing.
● Trace the bottle on page 71 and cut a template from thin card. Roll out some white modelling paste on a lightly greased board. Using template and scalpel, cut out bottle silhouette. Turn the book shaped cake tin (pan) upside down and place the bottle shape on it. Dampen the silhouette lightly with water. Pad it with paste, building up the bottle shape and smoothing the edges. Cut out a second silhouette, about 2.5mm ($\frac{1}{8}$ in) larger than the first, from white modelling paste. Dampen the bottle and apply the second silhouette, smoothing and stretching it slightly.
● Mask label area on bottle with greaseproof paper (parchment). Airbrush bottle with gooseberry green food colour. Remove masking paper. When bottle is dry, cut a piece of modelling paste to the size of the label, dampen back with water and attach it to the bottle. When dry, paint the design, using black food colour, and add the inscription L'Chaim. Attach bottle to the cake with royal icing.
● Make cork template (page 71). Colour some modelling paste light brown. Roll it out and, using template and scalpel, cut out cork silhouette. Dampen back of paste and apply to cake, smoothing edges to give cork a rounded appearance. When dry, paint the top silver.
● Make the bas relief bunnies on the inverted cake tin (pan), using the templates on page 71 and modelling paste in pastel colours. The technique is the same as that for the Easter bunny, see pages 30-31. Add skullcaps and shawls if liked. When dry, attach bunnies to cake with royal icing. Cut 2 strips of blue paste for book mark and fix in place. Highlight bunnies with dusting powder and give bottle a gloss by painting with confectioners' varnish. Finally pipe bubbles, using piping gel.

HEART ENGAGEMENT CAKE
WITH BAS RELIEF DOVES

*T*he technique for making the bas relief doves for this romantic cake is described in detail in step-by-step instructions on page 36-37.

23cm (9 in) heart shaped cake
apricot glaze
1.25kg (2½ lb) marzipan (almond paste)
1.5kg (3 lb) Royal Icing, see page 6
selection of food colourings
125g (4 oz) Modelling Paste, see page 8
small amount of Flower Paste, see page 6
14 sugar buds
20 sugar leaves
12 sugar blossoms
E Q U I P M E N T
36cm (14 in) cake board
scriber
airbrush
scalpel
veining tool
ball tool
no. 2, 1 and 0 piping tubes (tips)
heart and bird cutters

● Brush cake with apricot glaze and cover with marzipan (almond paste). Coat cake and board with royal icing. When final coat is dry, attach cake to board.

● Extension work is used on side of cake. Measure height and circumference of cake and make a greaseproof paper (parchment) template. Use a scriber to mark the lines for the bridge and the top of the extension work. Leave paper template in place to protect side of cake while airbrushing top with pale blue food colouring.

● Trace doves and branch, page 68, and scribe the design on the top of the cake. Scribe inscription. Make bas relief doves, following step-by-step instructions on pages 36-37. Using a no.2 tube (tip) and white royal icing, pipe rope border around top edge of cake. Overpipe border with a no. 1 tube and blue icing. Use same tube and icing to pipe inscription.

● Pipe the small lace pieces for the top line of extension work on wax paper. Use a no.0 tube (tip) and white royal icing. Make plenty of extra pieces to allow for breakages.

● Before commencing bridge work, pipe a small shell border around base of cake, using a no.1 tube (tip) and white royal icing. Mix enough blue icing to complete bridge as even a slight change in colour will show. Pipe bridge and allow it to dry before piping white extension lines (see Note).

● Colour some flower paste pink, roll it out on a lightly greased surface and cut out 4 small hearts with the cutter. Re-roll paste and cut out a ribbon for side of cake, as shown opposite. Trim end of each ribbon to a V-shape. Roll out some white flower paste and cut out 4 small birds. Attach ribbon to side of cake with dots of icing, as shown, adding birds and hearts at regular intervals. When attaching birds, position them so that wings and tails are lifted slightly away from the cake.

● Using dots of royal icing, carefully add lace pieces to top line of extension work. Attach sugar blossoms, buds and leaves to top and side of cake with royal icing.

NOTE Detailed instructions for piping the extension work are not included in this book as the technique is covered elsewhere in the *Sugarcraft Skills* Series.

Making the appliqué doves illustrated on previous page

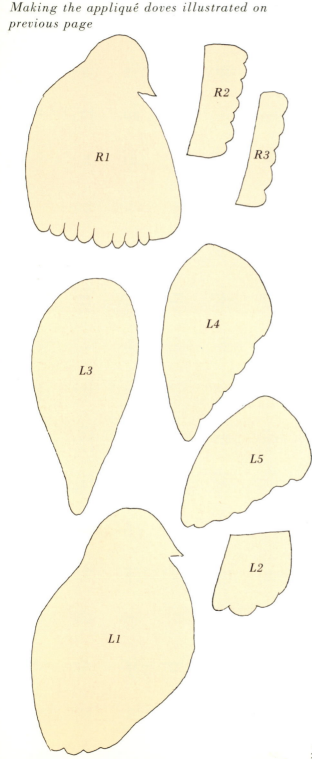

Trace doves on page 68 and scribe design on cake. Cut a card template of each bird, 2.5mm ($\frac{1}{8}$ in) smaller than tracings. Using templates, cut out bird silhouettes from white modelling paste. Dampen cake lightly; attach left bird. Roll rope of brown paste for twig. Flatten slightly, texture with veining tool and attach to cake.

Make card templates of dove head and body sections (L1 and R1 opposite). Roll out white modelling paste fairly thickly. Using templates and scalpel, cut out both head/body sections. Attach to birds on cake, smoothing edges to give a rounded effect. Texture feathers, smooth paste on right hand bird so that it overhangs the branch. Mark eye socket with ball tool.

~ 2 ~

Add right hand bird. Cut out small strips of paste for ends of tail feather strips and attach them to both silhouettes.

~ 3 ~

Make cardboard templates of upper tail feathers (L2, R2 and R3 opposite). Cut from white modelling paste; texture feathers with veining tool. Dampen backs of feathers and attach to bird silhouettes. Finish branch with a rope of brown modelling paste as shown, taking it across the right hand bird.

~ 5 ~

Make templates of wing sections for left hand bird (L3, L4 and L5) opposite. Cut wing sections from thinly rolled white paste; lightly texture them in a scallop design. Assemble wing by overlaying feathers and sticking sections together with water or egg white. Attach wing to bird, leaving one edge slightly raised.

~ 6 ~

Highlight texture of birds by painting them lightly with very pale grey food colouring. Paint beaks and eyes black. Attach sugar buds, leaves and blossoms.

18TH BIRTHDAY KEY CAKE

*S*tep-by-step instructions for making the bas relief pig are on pages 40-41.

15 x 20cm (6 x 8 in) oval cake
18cm (7 in) square cake
apricot glaze
1.5kg (3 lb) marzipan (almond paste)
1.75kg (3½ lb) Royal Icing, see page 6
selection of food colourings
125g (4 oz) Modelling Paste, see page 8
blue dusting powder (petal dust/blossom tint)
confectioners' varnish
E Q U I P M E N T
28 x 48cm (11 x 19 in) cake board
no. 1, 0, 44, 42 piping tubes (tips)
scriber
scalpel
needle tool
veining tool
1.5m (1²⁄₃ yd) blue ribbon

● Cut cakes to form the key shape, following the diagram right. Stick pieces together with apricot glaze, then brush cake with glaze and cover with marzipan (almond paste). Coat cake and board with several coats of royal icing, smoothing the surface with a straight edge and side scraper. When final coating is dry, place cake on coated cake board.

● Runout letters are used for the inscription (see Note). Write the letters and numerals clearly on a piece of card, secure wax paper on top and outline each letter using a no.1 tube (tip) and deep blue royal icing. Flood the inscription with run- icing in a lighter shade of blue. Place the runout inscription under a warm lamp to dry.

● Trace pig, page 40, and scribe the design on the cake. Complete the bas relief, following the step-by-step instructions on page 40-41.

● Pipe a shell border around the base of the cake,

using a no.44 piping tube (tip) and full peak white royal icing. Using the same tube, pipe the S-scrolls and shells for the top border. Overpipe scrolls using white icing and no.42 and 2 tubes. Complete the border by using a no.1 tube and blue icing to overpipe S-scrolls; pipe a dot between each shell.

● Place ribbon around side of cake, attaching it with dots of icing and ensuring that the join is at the back. Remove runout letters from wax paper; fix them to cake with a dot of icing. Finish cake by piping notes on top of cake, next to portable stereo. Use black royal icing and a no.1 piping tube (tip).

NOTE Detailed instructions for runouts are not included in this book as the technique is covered elsewhere in the *Sugarcraft Skills* Series.

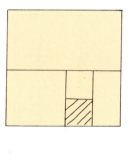

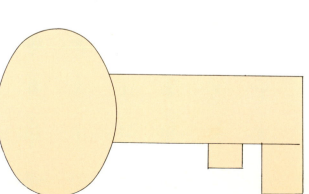

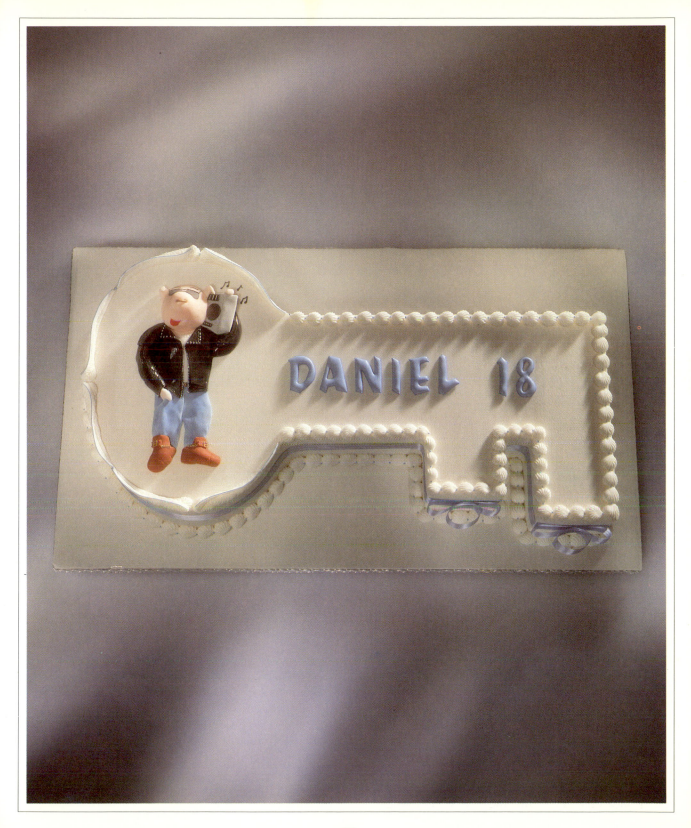

Making the bas relief pig illustrated on previous page

~ 1 ~

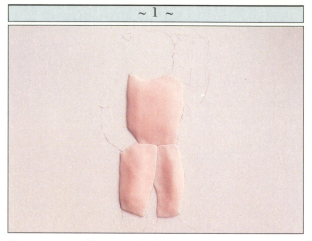

Trace pig silhouette left and scribe outline on cake. Trace clothing (page 71) and make cardboard template for each piece. Pad body. Cut out chest/T-shirt and legs from flesh-coloured modelling paste, making paste pieces slightly narrower than template. Taper edges, dampen backs of paste pieces and attach to cake.

~ 4 ~

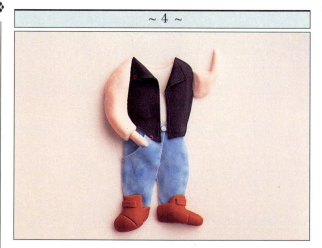

Cut out jacket fronts from black modelling paste. Dampen backs of paste pieces with water and attach jacket fronts to body, folding back the edge of paste to make lapels. Pad arms with flesh-coloured paste.

~ 2 ~

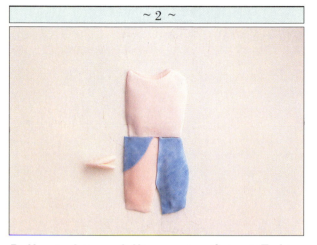

Roll out white modelling paste. Cut out T-shirt. Lightly dampen back of paste and fix shirt in position. Roll out pale blue paste; create a denim effect by brushing with blue dusting powder. Cut out pocket and left trouser leg. Fix in place, easing them over the padding. Model pig's trotter from flesh-coloured paste.

~ 3 ~

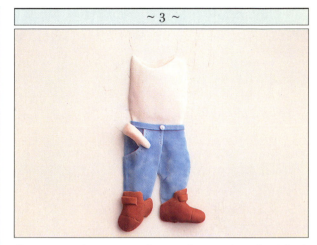

Cut out right trouser leg and waistband. Mark stitching along pocket and zip with needle tool, then dampen back of paste lightly and fix in position. Slide trotter into pocket before paste dries. Mould boots from chestnut brown paste, fix in place, then mark soles and heels with veining tool. Use paste strips for straps.

~ 5 ~

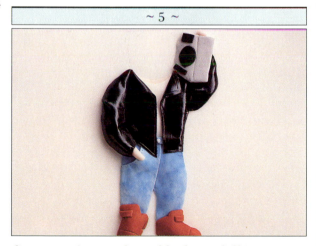

Cut out sleeves from black modelling paste. Dampen arms and tuck sleeves over them, making folds and creases where necessary. Glaze jacket with confectioners' varnish to create a leather effect. Make portable stereo from grey modelling paste. For the speaker, cut a round from black modelling paste, using end of a piping tube (tip).

~ 6 ~

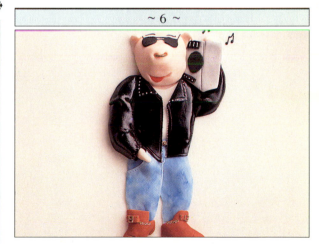

Mould pig's face and ears from flesh-coloured paste. Make a slit for the mouth with a scalpel. Mould tongue from red paste, dampen edges and insert in mouth. Attach face to cake. Make holes for nostrils, using the end of a paintbrush. Cut glasses from black paste and fix in place. Decorate jacket and boots as liked, using a no.0 tube (tip) and white royal icing.

MOTHER'S DAY CAKE
WITH BAS RELIEF COWBOY

*S*tep-by-step instructions for making the cowboy are on pages 44-45.

25 x 30cm (10 x 12 in) oval cake
apricot glaze
1.5kg (3 lb) marzipan (almond paste)
small amount of Royal Icing, see page 6
clear alcohol (gin or vodka)
2kg (4 lb) Sugarpaste, see page 24
125g (4 oz) Modelling Paste, see page 8
selection of food colourings
peach dusting powder (petal dust/blossom tint)
E Q U I P M E N T
30 x 36cm (12 x 14 in) oval cake board
crimper
scriber
cocktail stick (toothpick)
no.2 and 1 piping tubes (tips)
Garrett frill cutter
2.25m (2½ yd) x 2.5mm (⅛ in) wide pink ribbon for bows and board
medium plunger blossom cutter
scalpel
dressmakers' tracing wheel
wooden dowel
large star cutter for sheriff's badge
1.2m (1⅓ yd) lace to trim board

● Brush cake with apricot glaze and coat with marzipan (almond paste). Secure to board with royal icing. Brush cake with alcohol. Roll out sugarpaste and coat cake and board. Smooth sides, taking care not to damage sugarpaste on board. Trim off any excess paste with a sharp knife. Crimp edge of board while paste is still pliable, then allow cake and board to dry.
● The side of the cake is decorated with Garrett frills. Measure height and circumference of cake and make a greaseproof paper (parchment) template. Fold template into 8 equal sections. Draw a shallow curve on each for the frills and draw circlets of flowers as shown opposite. Attach paper template to side of cake. Scribe curves. Do not scribe circlets; instead pin centre position of each tiny flower, using a pin or needle tool. Remove template.
● Pipe a small shell border around base of cake, using a no.2 tube (tip) and white royal icing. Using the cutter, lemon and white sugarpaste and the cocktail stick (toothpick), make the Garrett frills (see Note). Moisten the marked line on the cake with a damp brush and quickly attach frills, gently lifting them with a soft dry brush to create a delicate effect. Neaten top edge of frills with a shell piped with a no.1 tube and white royal icing.
● Make 8 small ribbon bows and attach one to the top of each frill with royal icing. Using the blossom cutter and modelling paste in pastel shades, make about 116 blossoms. Set aside about 20 blossoms and use the rest for the circlets of flowers on the side of the cake, attaching them with dots of icing. Pipe a centre to each blossom using white royal icing and a no.1 tube (tip). Using green or white royal icing and a no.1 tube, pipe shells to represent leaves between blossoms.
● Make bas relief cowboy directly on the surface of the cake, following instructions on pages 44-45. Pipe inscription using a no.2 tube (tip) and royal icing in a variety of bright colours. Pipe grass at cowboy's feet, using green icing and a no.1 tube. Using the same icing and tube, pipe flower stems. Attach reserved flowers to cake with dots of icing, remembering to place some at cowboy's feet and giving others the appearance of having fallen off their stems. Trim board with ribbon and lace.
NOTE Detailed instructions for making the Garrett frills are not included in this book as the technique is covered elsewhere in the *Sugarcraft Skills* Series.

Making the bas relief cowboy illustrated on previous page

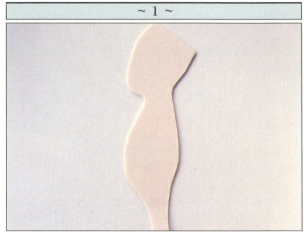

~ 1 ~

Trace cowboy silhouette opposite. Cut a template of the basic body shape from thin card, about 2.5mm ($\frac{1}{8}$ in) smaller all round than the tracing. Roll out some white or flesh coloured modelling paste on a lightly greased board. Cut out body shape. Lightly dampen back of paste with water and secure it to cake.

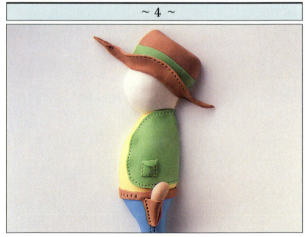

~ 4 ~

Continue dressing figure, adding waistcoat (with pocket) and holster. Mark stitch marks in paste pieces before attaching them to figure if possible. When attaching hat brim, dampen edge and secure firmly to crown. Brim will flop over cowboy's face. Turn back when firmly attached to create a neat fold with no visible cut edges. Mould gun and fix in holster.

~ 2 ~

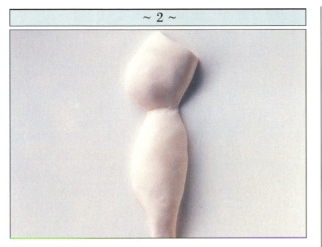

Trace clothing and face on page 69 and make card templates of each piece. Note that clothes are wider than body silhouette but not longer. Build up figure with white or flesh coloured paste, stretching paste over silhouette and smoothing edges. Cut face shape from paste. dampen back lightly and attach to figure.

~ 3 ~

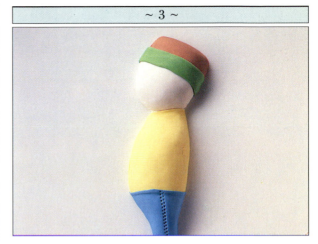

Dress figure: Using template, scalpel and yellow modelling paste, cut out shirt (pattern will be added later). Dampen paste; fix shirt in position. Do not make sleeve at this stage. Make crown of hat from brown paste and band from green. Fix in position. Cut out trousers from blue paste; mark seam with *tracing wheel*. Attach to figure.

~ 5 ~

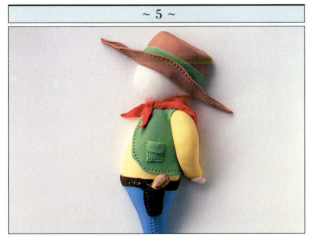

Model hand (see page 9) and allow to dry. Make sleeve from yellow paste, hollowing cuff with dowel. Dampen inside of cuff lightly with water and insert hand. Dampen back of sleeve and attach to body. Cut kerchief from red paste, making bow from two pointed strips of paste covered with a small knot. Fix in place.

~ 6 ~

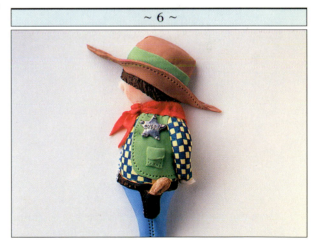

Mould cowboy's nose from flesh coloured paste and blush cheeks with peach dusting powder. Pipe hair with brown royal icing and a no.1 tube (tip), using a damp paintbrush to blend strands together. Paint checks and finishing details on shirt, belt and holster. Cut out a paste star for sheriff badge, fix it in place and paint silver.

STRAWBERRY FAIRY CAKE

*S*tep-by-step instructions for making the strawberry fairy are on pages 48-49.

20cm (8 in) round cake
apricot glaze
750g (1½ lb) marzipan (almond paste)
1.25kg (2½ lb) Sugarpaste, see page 24
selection of food colourings
clear alcohol (gin or vodka)
small amount of Royal Icing, see page 6
Flower Paste, see page 6
125g (4 oz) Modelling Paste, see page 8
dusting powder (petal dust/blossom tint) in
various colours
7 wired sugar strawberries
20 sugar rose leaves
12 wired sugar strawberry blossoms
E Q U I P M E N T
28cm (11 in) round cake board
scriber
no. 2, 1 and 0 piping tubes (tips)
scalpel
rose petal, leaf and calyx cutters
ball tool
veining tool
cocktail stick (toothpick)
1m (1 yd 3 in) ribbon to trim board

● Brush cake with apricot glaze and coat with marzipan (almond paste). Colour sugarpaste with gooseberry green food colouring, then roll it out. Cover board. Brush cake with alcohol and cover with sugarpaste, smoothing top and sides. Allow cake and board to dry separately for three days.

● Using royal icing, attach cake to board, offsetting it slightly from the centre to allow room for the spray of strawberries on the right hand side.

● Extension work is used on side of cake. Measure height and circumference of cake and make a greaseproof paper (parchment) template. Fold template into 12 equal sections. Draw a scallop design on 10 sections, leaving two plain to accommodate a spray of strawberries as shown. Scribe the design on the side of the cake.

● Using a no.2 tube (tip) and white royal icing, pipe a small shell border around base of cake. Pipe curved bridge work using a no.1 tube. Allow bridge to dry completely before piping extension lines, see Note, page 34. Neaten top edge with dropped loops and embroidery, using a no.1 tube, extending the design over the plain sections.

● Paint background on top of cake with food colouring. Brush embroidery (pages 14-15) may be used on some of the leaves to create dimension.

Continued on page 48

Continued from page 46

● Make bas relief directly on the surface of the cake, following instructions opposite. Attach sprays of strawberries, leaves and blossoms **to** top and side of cake with royal icing, taking care that wires do not penetrate the sugarpaste coating.

● Complete cake with inscription and 'dot' embroidery, using a no. 0 tube and deep gooseberry green royal icing. Trim board with ribbon.

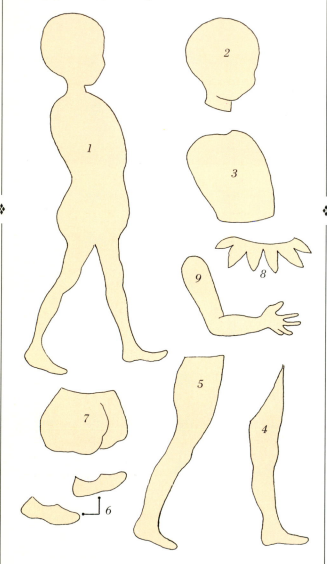

~ 1 ~

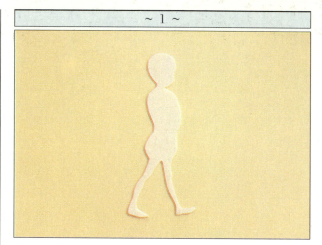

Trace fairy sections opposite and cut templates from thin card. Roll out a small amount of white modelling paste on a lightly greased board. Using template 1 and scalpel, cut out the silhouette of the figure. Dampen back of paste lightly with water and position it on cake.

~ 4 ~

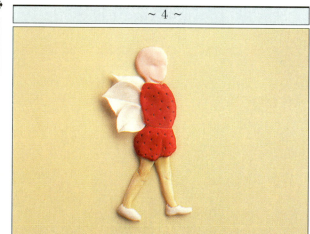

Roll out some red modelling paste, slightly thicker than the white. Using templates 3 and 7, cut out tunic and trousers. Attach both to the figure, gently blending edges over silhouette. Use cocktail stick (toothpick) to prick small holes into which the pips will be piped. Cut out and attach the white shoes, using templates 6.

~ 2 ~

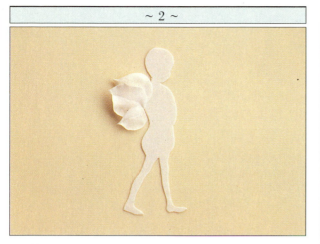

Roll out white flower paste thinly, then cut out 2 medium and 1 small rose petal for wings. Smooth edge of each petal with a ball tool and mark centre lines with a veining tool. Attach medium petals to fairy first, carefully overlapping them to give the appearance of wings.

~ 3 ~

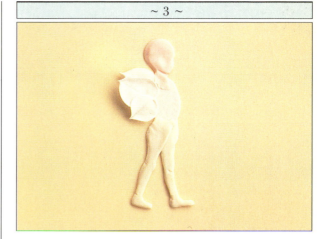

Lightly pad forehead and cheek with white modelling paste, shaping it with the wide end of the veining tool. Using flesh coloured paste, template 2 and scalpel, cut out head. Mark neck. Cut out and attach back leg(5), smooth edges; attach front leg (4). Use a little green dusting powder to add shape to the legs.

~ 5 ~

Paint face and hair. Blush cheeks with dusting powder. Make dark green cap, taking template from sketch on page 46. Fix it in place; roll front petals back. Make green paste trim at waist and neckline, using template 8; fix in place. Model four strawberries; cut out two pale green leaves for 'basket'. Fix in place. Pipe pips on tunic with yellow icing and no.0 tube (tip).

~ 6 ~

Model arm and hand (see page 9) and attach to body. Cut a small white rose petal for the sleeve, smoothing the edge before fixing it in place. Cut out two small green calyxes to trim the shoes. Fix them in place, then pipe centres, using yellow royal icing and a no.1 tube (tip). Lightly dust wings and hat with pale green/brown colour to bring figure to life.

CLOWN PLAQUE

125g (4 oz) Sugarpaste, see page 24
90g (3 oz) Modelling Paste, see page 8
selection of food colourings
white vegetable fat (shortening)
pink dusting powder (petal dust/blossom tint)
E Q U I P M E N T
18cm (7 in) round cake board
button or embossing tool
scalpel
veining tool
cocktail stick (toothpick)
small pieces of foam
clay gun

● Make plaque by covering board with sugarpaste, trimming edge neatly. While paste is supple, emboss edge of plaque, using button or embossing tool. Trace clown right. Cut one thin card template of the silhouette and individual templates of the clothing. Roll out flesh coloured modelling paste on a lightly greased board. Using template and scalpel, cut out clown silhouette, dampen back and attach to plaque.

● Lightly pad cheeks with two small balls of flesh coloured paste, shaping them with the wide end of the veining tool. Cut out face from flesh coloured paste and position over padding, smoothing the edges neatly.

● Cut a strip of thinly rolled white paste and frill one side with a cocktail stick (toothpick). Pleat the paste, see page 9, to make the ruffle. Attach to the neck so that the ruffle covers the face. Quickly cut out yellow tunic and attach, then turn the frill down; this prevents a cut edge from showing round the neck.

● Model hands, see page 9. Frill two strips of white paste for cuffs. Fix hands and cuffs in position.

● Cut shoes from yellow paste. Fix in position before cutting out blue trousers. Lightly dampen top of shoes and attach trousers, using the same method as for the neck frill to avoid visible join.

To create the characteristic baggy shape, place foam pieces in the trousers to hold the paste until dry. Cut braces from lilac paste and attach them with royal icing.

● Soften a little lilac paste with vegetable fat (shortening) and extrude a little for bobble on hat (see page 8). Cut out hat from yellow paste and fix in position. Soften a little orange modelling paste with vegetable fat and extrude hair. Blush cheeks with pink dusting powder, then paint eyes before modelling ball-shaped nose and sausage-shaped mouth. Paint stripes or dots on trousers, tunic and hat. Paint shoes, add shoe laces and buttons.

CHRISTENING CAKE FOR TWINS

*T*his delightful cake can easily be adapted for a single baby - or even quads! Instructions for the cradle and twins are on pages 54-55.

20cm (8 in) round cake
apricot glaze
1kg (2 lb) marzipan (almond paste)
clear alcohol (gin or vodka)
1kg (2 lb) Sugarpaste, see page 24
small amount of Royal Icing, see page 6
125g (4 oz) Modelling Paste, see page 8
selection of food colourings
white vegetable fat (shortening)
cornflour (cornstarch)
E Q U I P M E N T
28cm (11 in) round cake board
scallop edge cutter
1m (1 yd 3 in) each x 2.5mm (¹⁄₈ in) wide
pink and blue ribbon
no. 2 and 1 piping tubes (tips)
medium plunger blossom cutter
scriber
scalpel
clay gun fitted with large trefoil top
Fimo modelling clay (available from art and
hobby shops)
small plastic teddy bear or doll
dressmakers' tracing wheel
round Garrett frill cutter

● Brush cake with apricot glaze and cover with marzipan. Brush with alcohol and coat with white sugarpaste, smoothing top and sides. Use remaining sugarpaste to cover board, scalloping edge with cutter. Allow sugarpaste to dry, then attach cake to coated board with royal icing.
● Measure height and circumference of cake and make a greaseproof paper (parchment) template. Fold template into eight equal sections, then fold template in half lengthwise to mark the centre of

each of the parallel folds. Secure template around cake and make a small pin hole to mark the centre of each fold. Remove template.
● Using template as a guide, cut lengths of pink and blue ribbon for the sides of the cake. Secure them around the base with dots of royal icing. Using no.2 tube (tip) and white icing, pipe a small shell border below the ribbon. Decorate the board by piping a loop of icing around the edge of each scallop, using a no.1 tube and white icing.
● Using the blossom cutter and modelling paste in pastel shades, cut out 48 medium blossoms, attaching these to the side of the cake in six groups with eight blossoms in each. To create a symmetrical design, place one flower on either side of each pin hole, then add three blossoms on each side. Scribe inscription on cake, then pipe lettering, using a no.1 tube (tip) and pink and blue icing.
● Make the bas relief cradle directly on the surface of the cake, following the instructions on pages 54-55. When cradle is complete, paint pattern on blanket and attach bows as shown opposite.

EXPERT ADVICE
≈
If no clay gun is available, create the rope effect by twisting two ropes of modelling paste together. Make sure that the ribbon joins are at the back of the cake.

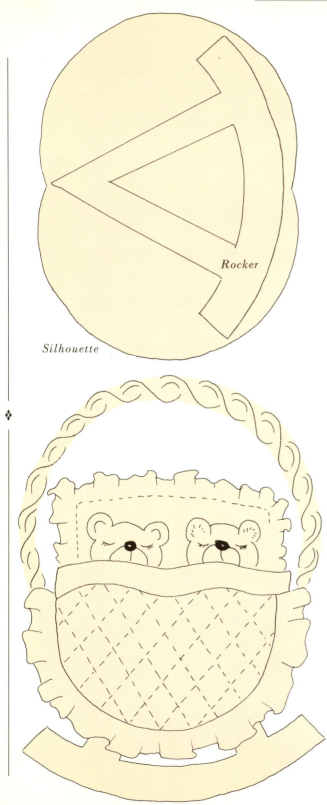

Silhouette

Rocker

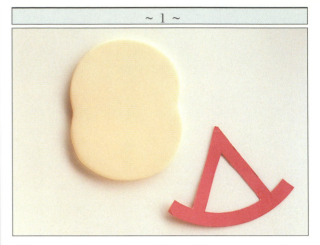

Trace rocker and cradle silhouette templates opposite and cut both out of thin card. Colour some modelling paste cream then cut out cradle silhouette with scalpel. Dampen back of paste and attach to cake. Marble some white modelling paste by blending in a little brown food colouring, roll it out and cut out the rocker. Let dry.

The easiest way to make the teddy bears is by first making a mould. Knead Fimo until pliable. Lightly grease the face of a plastic teddy or doll of suitable size, press into the Fimo, then remove plastic figure. If impression is clear, bake Fimo following manufacturer's instructions. If impression is poor, re-knead Fimo and try again.

~ 2 ~

Secure rocker to cradle base with royal icing. Soften some cream modelling paste with vegetable fat (shortening) and extrude it through the clay gun (see page 8), twisting paste to form a rope. Attach rope to top of cradle.

~ 3 ~

Build up bottom edge of cradle: Extrude two more lengths of paste from the clay gun, each about 15cm (6 in) in length. Dampen bottom edge of cradle silhouette and secure one rope on top of the other to create height. Trim off any excess paste.

~ 5 ~

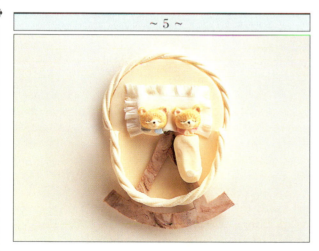

Lightly dust a small ball of cream paste with cornflour (cornstarch); press into mould. Remove at once and trim off excess paste. Paint features with food colouring. Cut out pillow from a piece of white paste. Pleat edge with cocktail stick (toothpick), dampen back of paste; fix in place. Position teddy faces and model bodies from cream paste.

~ 6 ~

Make blanket from blue paste, creating quilted effect with dressmakers' tracing wheel. Place a strip of white paste along top edge for sheet. Cut a Garrett frill from pink paste, frill edge with a cocktail stick (toothpick) and attach to edge of blanket to hide ropes of paste.

TIERED WEDDING CAKE

A heart shaped cake is assembled over an oval one to create a stunning effect.

15cm (6 in) heart shaped cake and 25 x 30cm
(10 x 12 in) oval cake
apricot glaze
2.25 kg (4½ lb) marzipan (almond paste)
small quantity of Flower Paste, see page 6
clear alcohol (gin or vodka)
3 kg (6½ lb) Sugarpaste, see page 24
selection of food colourings
pink lustre dusting powder
(petal dust/blossom tint)
small quantity of Royal Icing, see page 6
125g (4 oz) Modelling Paste, see page 8
8 sugar roses; 80 small sugar blossoms;
4 sugar leaves
EQUIPMENT
dowel
20cm (8 in) heart shaped cake board
and 25 x 30cm (10 x 12 in) oval cake board
2cm (¾ in) chisel brush
no.2, 0 and 1 piping tubes (tips)
scalpel
ball tool
veining tool
perspex (Plexiglass) tilting cake stand

● Brush both cakes with apricot glaze and coat with marzipan (almond paste). Leave to dry. Roll out some flower paste on a lightly greased board and cut out eighty 2.5mm x 8mm (⅛ x ⅜ in) sugar ribbon strips. Wrap strips over lightly greased dowel to dry. Make a thin card template for top of each cake, so that ribbon pieces can be inserted symmetrically. Each template should be same shape as cake, but 5cm (2 in) smaller all round.
● Brush cakes with alcohol. Cover with cream coloured sugarpaste. Immediately place heart-shaped template on the smaller cake. Insert sugar strips evenly all around it, anchoring ends in soft paste, see Note. Repeat procedure on oval cake. Remove templates. Coat boards in sugarpaste; dry.
● Measure height and circumference of cakes and make a greaseproof paper (parchment) template for each. Fold each template into eight equal sections and cut the bottom of the template into scallops, making one scallop on the oval cake deeper than the rest to accommodate the brides-maid. Attach templates to cakes so that they mask the upper portion of each side. Using chisel brush apply pink lustre dusting powder to exposed areas underneath. Remove templates and secure cakes to coated boards with royal icing.
● Pipe a small shell border around the base of each cake, using white royal icing and a no.2 piping tube (tip). Using a no.0 tube, pipe 220 lace motifs on wax paper, see Note. When dry, attach motifs to both cakes with royal icing, just above the dusting powder line. Again using a no. 0 tube, pipe tiny dots between sugar ribbon strips.
● Attach sugar flowers and leaves to oval cake. Fix three blossoms on sides of cake at top of each scallop, then, using a no.0 tube (tip) and pale green royal icing, pipe shells to represent leaves.
● Make bas relief figures, using the templates on page 68. The technique is the same as that used for the strawberry fairy (see pages 48-49). The bridal pair are made directly on the cake; the bridesmaid is made separately and attached with royal icing when dry. Using white icing and a no.1 tube (tip), pipe bride's veil. Gently brush lines with a damp paintbrush for a delicate effect.
● If heart shaped top tier is to be tilted, glue a small piece of plastic angle strip (90°) to back of board. This rests on stand to stop cake sliding off.
NOTE Detailed instructions for ribbon insertion and lace making are not included in this book as the techniques are covered elsewhere in the *Sugarcraft Skills* Series.

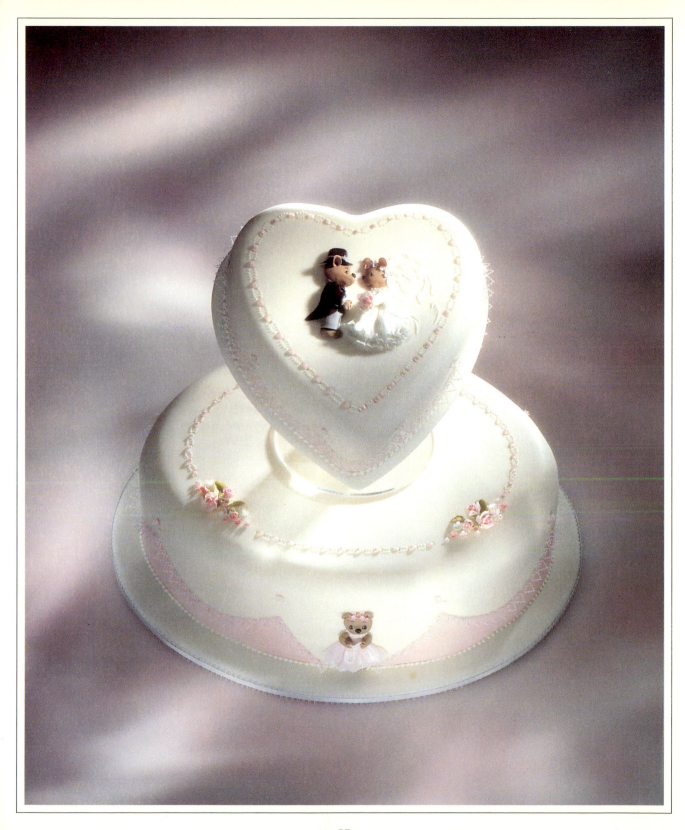

CHRISTMAS CAKE
WITH BAS RELIEF FIGURES

Once the skills of bas relief and appliqué have been mastered, they may be combined with other elements to produce interesting effects. This cake demonstrates how to create dimension by overlay. Instructions for the detail on top of the cake are on pages 60-61.

18cm (7 in) round cake
apricot glaze
1kg (2 lb) marzipan (almond paste)
1.25kg (2½ lb) Royal Icing, see page 6
selection of food colourings
30g (1 oz) Modelling Paste, see page 8
E Q U I P M E N T
30cm (12 in) square cake board
no. 2, 1 and 0 piping tubes (tips)
scalpel
airbrush
scriber
cranked pallet knife
small piece of foam
cocktail sticks (toothpicks)
1.5m (1²/₃ yd) ribbon to trim board

● Brush cake with apricot glaze and cover with marzipan (almond paste) and royal icing. Coat the cake board with royal icing, applying several coats to obtain a good surface. Allow to dry.

● Make cardboard template for collar, following instructions on page 66. Place template on coated board. Pipe graduated line work around outside edge of template, using no.2, 1 and 0 tubes (tips), piping the outer edge with a no.0 tube and red icing. Secure the coated cake to the board, using a small amount of royal icing.

● Using a no.1 tube (tip) and green royal icing, pipe about 12 holly leaves on wax paper (the best eight will be used on the collar). Place paper on a gently curving surface to dry.

● Attach collar template to a firm, flat board.

Tape wax paper on top, keeping paper taut, so that no ripples appear. Outline collar using a no.1 tube (tip) and white royal icing, then run out collar with softened icing, see Note, page 38. Use a brush to ease icing into position. Cut a cross in centre of wax paper with a scalpel; this will help to release tension as icing dries and will prevent collar from cracking. Allow collar to dry in a warm place.

● Remove collar from wax paper. Pipe a green scallop around cut-out section, using a no.1 tube (tip) and royal icing. Attach holly leaves with a dot of icing. Pipe berries, using a no.1 tube and red icing. Set collar aside.

● The design on the side of the cake (not visible in photograph) consists of four holly wreaths, made as for wreath on top of cake and spaced an equal distance apart so that when collar is attached to cake, they may be glimpsed through cut-outs. On either side of each holly wreath is a panel outlined in line piping, with a design of piped greenery (like that above door on top of cake) and runout lanterns (template on page 60). Follow suggestions above, or work out your own design.

● Finish side of cake with a small shell border on the base line, using a no. 2 tube (tip). Decorate top of cake, following instructions on pages 60-61.

● When complete, attach runout collar; finish by piping three lines of graduated piping to match piping on board.

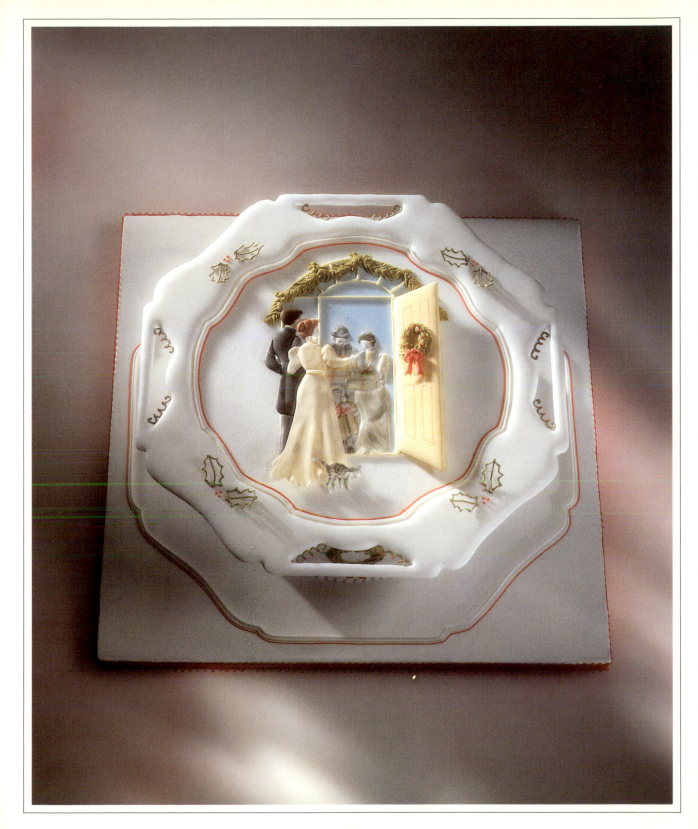

Decorating the top of the Christmas cake illustrated on previous page

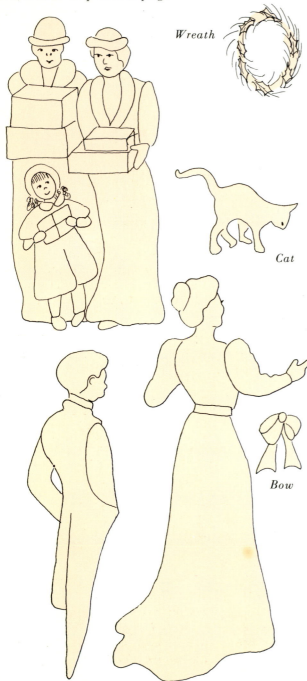

Wreath

Cat

Bow

~ 1 ~

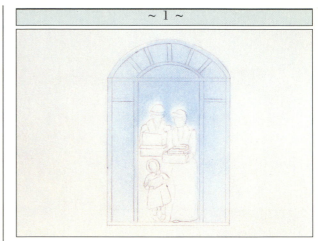

Trace templates (opposite and on page 66); cut out of thin card. Make a greaseproof paper (parchment) template for the top of the cake; cut out door arch. Place on cake and airbrush arch area with light blue colour. Trace door frame and guests on both sides of a sheet of tracing paper; scribe on airbrushed area.

~ 4 ~

Trace host, cat and holly wreath (opposite) and door (page 66). Run out on wax paper; allow to dry. Carefully remove all runouts except cat from paper, using the cranked palette knife. Paint detail on runouts, then attach to cake with royal icing, placing a small piece of foam under door to support it until icing is dry.

~ 2 ~

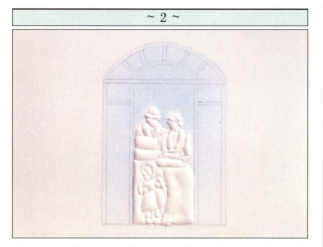

Run out figures of guests directly on the cake with white royal icing. Begin by flooding the areas which appear furthest away. Take care not to flood two adjacent sections without waiting for the first to crust over, or icing will blend together and definition will be lost.

~ 3 ~

Pipe door frame using white royal icing and a no.2 tube (tip), omitting the side where the door is to be attached. Using green icing and no.1 tube, pipe greenery over door, working one section at a time. Use a damp paintbrush to smooth the icing out from the centre. Paint detail on runout guests.

~ 5 ~

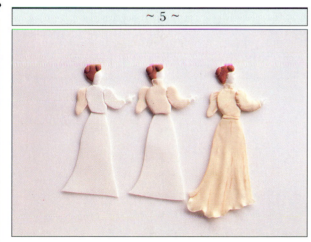

Using hostess template and scalpel, cut silhouette from white modelling paste. Run out face, hair and hand on silhouette; allow to dry. Cut out clothing in sections from cream paste, making shapes slightly wider than templates. Pad chest and forearm on silhouette; frill collar and attach clothes to figure, see Note right. Paint hair and shading on skirt.

~ 6 ~

When bas relief figure of hostess is dry, attach to cake with royal icing, placing the figure so that she slightly overlaps the runout host. Attach runout cat with royal icing.
NOTE When dressing hostess figure, place small cocktail sticks (toothpicks) under skirt for pleated effect.

TUXEDO PLAQUE

*I*f enlarged, this plaque would make a most attractive novelty cake for a man. Double the quantity of sugarpaste for a cake.

125g (4 oz) Sugarpaste, see page 24
black and silver food colouring
1 sugar carnation
E Q U I P M E N T
10 x 12.5cm (4 x 5 in) cake board
round Garrett frill cutter
scalpel
cocktail sticks (toothpicks)

● Trace tuxedo right and make a thin card template of the silhouette. Make individual templates of the various parts. Cut board to same shape as silhouette and cover with sugarpaste.
● Using cutter, cut out two Garrett frills (see Note, page 42). Frill edge of each with a cocktail stick (toothpick). Attach to the covered board with water, as shown right. Cut another paste strip wide enough to cover the inner edge of each frill. Fix it in place. Before frills dry, cut out and attach collar so that it lies neatly against shirt.
● Make cummerbund from three strips of paste, attaching it to the plaque as shown right. Colour some paste black and roll it out. Using templates and scalpel, cut out jacket and lapels. Dampen backs lightly and attach pieces carefully to shirt, taking care not to stretch paste.
● Make bow tie from black paste and attach it in the same way. Lastly make buttons from four small balls of white sugarpaste. When buttons are dry, paint with silver food colour and attach to shirt with royal icing. To finish the plaque, attach sugar carnation.

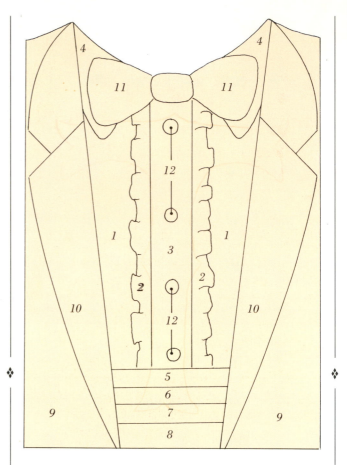

> ### EXPERT ADVICE
> ≈
> Do not roll sugarpaste too thin or the layer beneath may show through.

APPLIQUE LETTERS

*L*arge letters or numerals make interesting and novel designs that can be adapted for a wide variety of occasions. Any of the bas relief or appliqué techniques in this book may be used for the decoration. Alternatively, find a picture to suit the occasion and design your own letter around it.

Begin by tracing the letter and motif on separate sheets of paper. Place the letter over the motif and move the paper about, trying several positions. When you are happy with the result, trace the motif on the letter. You may need to reduce or enlarge the letter or motif if they do not fit well together, or use a different style of letter.

Using one of the templates opposite or on pages 66 or 67, or working from your own design, cut out a card template. Roll out some flower paste (not too thinly) on a lightly greased board. Using template and scalpel, cut out letter and motif, trimming away any excess paste. Carefully lift letter and motif onto cake or plaque, taking care not to distort the shape of the letter.

If letter is to be coloured with dusting powder or by airbrushing, allow it to dry on a board lightly dusted with cornflour (cornstarch). This will prevent paste from sticking. Colour it when dry, then attach to cake or plaque with royal icing.

Smaller letters or numerals may be made by using a mould (see page 7): Knead some vegetable fat (shortening) into a piece of flower paste. Take a small piece of paste and push it firmly into the clean dry mould. Trim away excess paste with a sharp knife, working first from the centre up, then from the centre down, to avoid dragging paste and distorting the letter. Remove letter immediately from mould, easing it out from the thickest part first. Position letter or letters on cake; secure with royal icing.

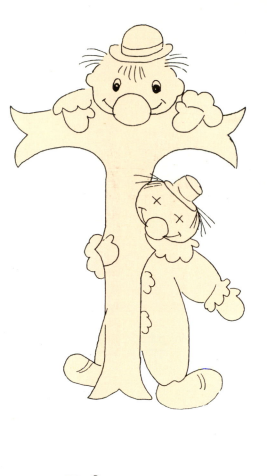

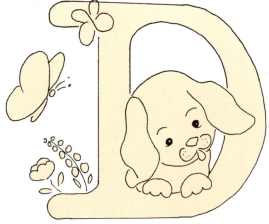

— *1*

— *2*

— *3*

Christmas Cake with Bas Relief Figures

Letter Plaque

Letter Plaque

— *4*

Collar template
Cut out a 28cm (11 in)
diameter circle on a piece
of paper, then fold into 8.
Trace template for collar,
place it on a segment on
circle and cut round curved
edge. Open paper up to
reveal template. Transfer it
on to thin card.

Anemones

Happy Birthday

Daffodils

Pansies

Daffodil Parts

Letter Plaque

Roses

67

Wedding Cake Figures

Heart Engagement Cake

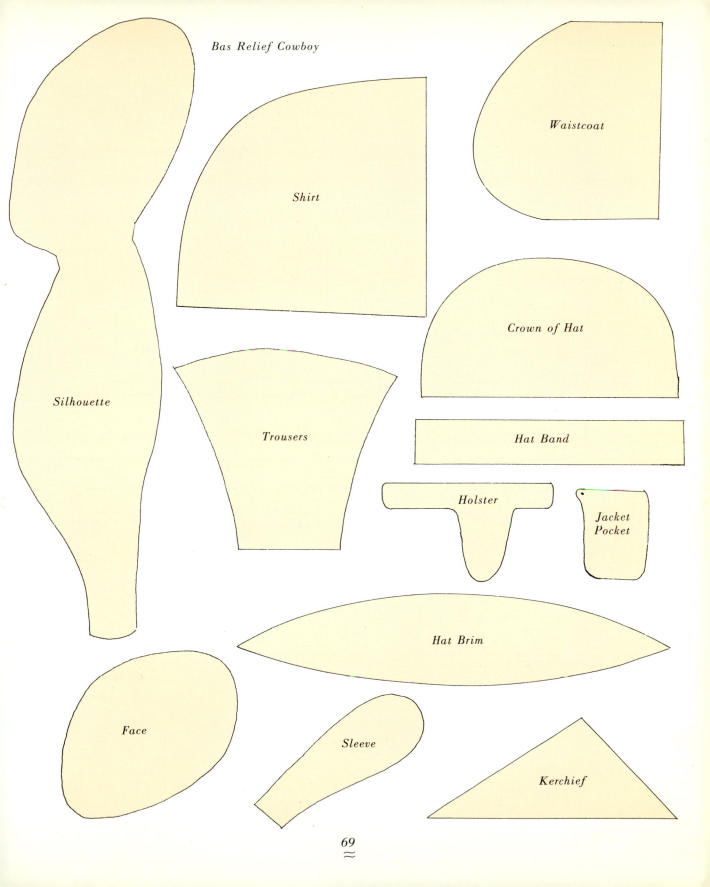

Bas Relief Cowboy

Silhouette

Shirt

Waistcoat

Trousers

Crown of Hat

Hat Band

Holster

Jacket Pocket

Hat Brim

Face

Sleeve

Kerchief

69

Rocking Horse Figure

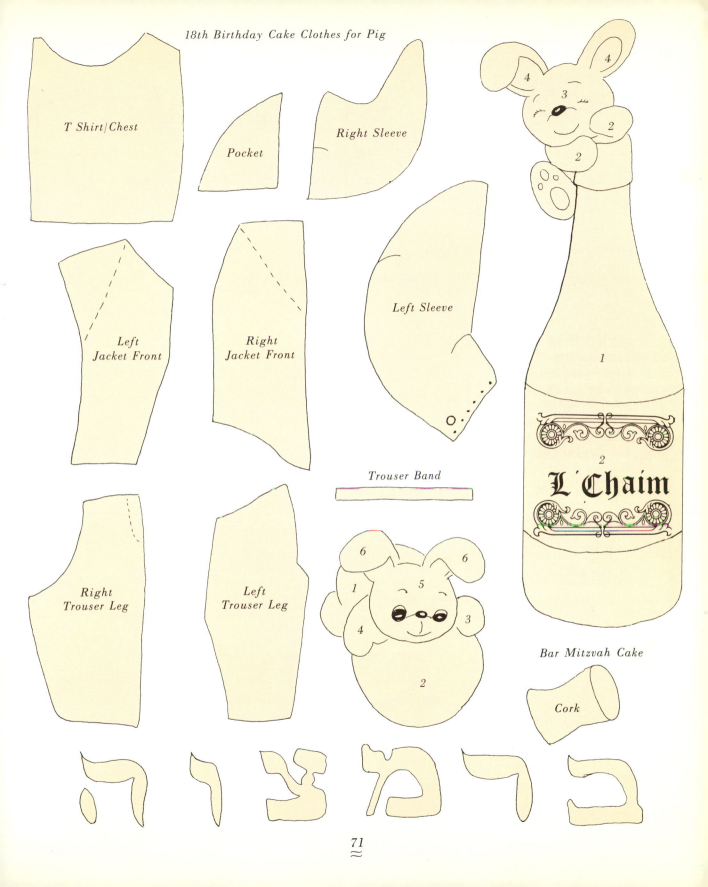

18th Birthday Cake Clothes for Pig

T Shirt/Chest

Pocket

Right Sleeve

Left Jacket Front

Right Jacket Front

Left Sleeve

Trouser Band

L'Chaim

Right Trouser Leg

Left Trouser Leg

Bar Mitzvah Cake

Cork

INDEX

FOR FURTHER INFORMATION

Merehurst is the leading publisher of cake decorating books and has an excellent range of titles to suit all levels. Please send for our free catalogue, stating the title of this book:

United Kingdom
*Marketing Department
Merehurst Ltd.
Ferry House
51-57 Lacy Road
London SW15 1PR
Tel: 081 780 1177
Fax: 081 780 1714*

U.S.A.
*Sterling Publishing Co. Inc.
387 Park Avenue South
New York
NY 10016-8810, USA
Tel: (1) 212 532 7160
Fax: (1) 212 213 2495*

Australia
*J.B. Fairfax Press Pty. Ltd.
80 McLachlan Avenue
Rushcutters Bay
NSW 2011
Tel: (61) 2 361 6366
Fax: (61) 2 360 6262*

Other Territories
*For further information contact:
International Sales Department at United Kingdom address.*